The material was previously published in the
book *Fearless Fair Isle Knitting 30 Gorgeous
Original Sweaters, Socks, Mittens, and More.*
(ISBN 978-1-60085-327-2)

First published in this format 2012.

 The Taunton Press
Inspiration for hands-on living®

The Taunton Press, Inc.
63 South Main Street, PO Box 5506
Newtown, CT 06470-5506

e-mail: tp@taunton.com

Interior Design and Layout:
Chalkley Calderwood
Illustrator: Christine Erikson
Photographers: Alexandra Grablewski; except
pp. 25–31 © Nick Pharris

Printed in the United States of America
10 9 8 7 6 5 4 3 2 1

Table of Contents

Floppy Hat

An autumn colorway is warm and glowing knit in the Geometric Dazzle motif. This straight-top, floppy hat, sized from toddler to adult, is an easy stranded project that even beginners can complete. (Shown at left knit in Knit Picks® Telemark yarn.)

Yarn	Light Weight Yarn (CYCA 3), approx. 100 yd. each of Green, Rust, Gold, Gray, and Black
Yarn Weight	Sport, Light (CYCA 3)
Needles	Size 5 (U.S.)/3.75 mm 16-in. circular, or size needed to obtain gauge
	Large-eye blunt needle, stitch markers

Pattern Sizes	Toddler (Child, Youth, Adult Small, Adult Large)
Measurements	Hat Length: 6 in. (6 in., 7 in., 8 in., 9 in.); Hat Circumference (unstretched) 15 in. (16¼ in., 17½ in. 18¾ in., 20 in.)
Pattern Difficulty	Easy
Fair Isle Gauge	6.5 sts = 1 in., 8 rnds = 1 in. on size 5 needles
Note	*See Taking the Fear Out of Fair Isle, page 23 for stranding instructions.*

Knitting Instructions

With Gold and 16-in. size 5 circular needle, CO 100 (108, 116, 124, 132) sts. Making sure that the sts are not twisted, join.

RNDS 1-6

Work K1, P1 ribbing.

RND 7

K.

Begin **Geometric Dazzle Floppy Hat and Reversible Scarf Chart** at Rnd 1. Work even, following chart, until hat measures 5⅞ in. (5⅞ in., 6⅞ in., 7⅞ in., 8⅞ in.) long.

NEXT RND

K with Gold.

BIND-OFF

Divide sts evenly on either side of the circular needle, and work a three-needle bind-off with Gold.

Weave all ends in on the inside of the hat. Wash and block hat.

Geometric Dazzle Floppy Hat and Reversible Scarf Chart

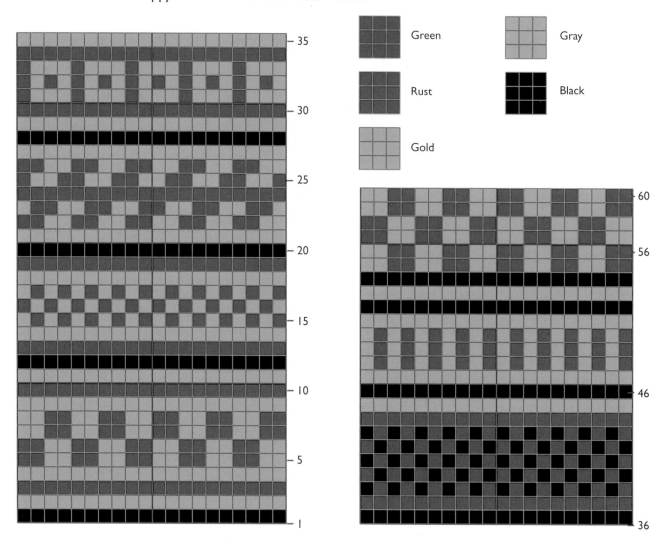

Reversible Scarf

This skinny, reversible scarf, a companion to the *Geometric Dazzle Floppy Hat*, is worked lengthwise in a circle, then cut open and closed with a bind-off that eliminates the need for a long seam. (Shown at left knit in Knit Picks Telemark™ yarn.)

Yarn	Light Weight Yarn (CYCA 3), approx. 100 yd. each of Green, Rust, Gold, Gray, and Black	**Pattern Size**	One size fits all
		Measurements	3¾ in. wide, 52 in. long
Yarn Weight	Sport, Light (CYCA 3)	**Pattern Difficulty**	Easy
Needles	Size 6 (U.S.)/4 mm 29-in. circular, or size needed to obtain gauge Large-eye blunt needle, stitch markers	**Fair Isle Gauge**	5.75 sts = 1 in., 7 rnds = 1 in. on size 6 needles
		Note	*See Taking the Fear Out of Fair Isle, page 23 for stranding instructions.*

Knitting Instructions

With Gold and 29-in. size 6 circular needle, CO 300 sts. Making sure that the sts are not twisted, place marker, join.

RND 1 K.

Begin **Geometric Dazzle Floppy Hat and Reversible Scarf Chart** (page 4) at Rnd 1. Work even, following chart, for the first 2 motif borders. Skip the next border, and then work the chart for the next 3 borders.

NEXT RND K with Gold.

Following instructions for reinforcing steeks (Taking the Fear Out of Fair Isle, page 29), reinforce the scarf at the beginning of the rnd, and cut the scarf open between the reinforcement stitching.

BIND-OFF Folding the scarf so that the WS is out, pick up a loop from the first cast-on st and place it on the left needle. K the loop and the st together. Pick up a loop from the next cast-on st and place it on the left needle. K the loop and that st together, then pass the st from the left needle over the most recent st.

Rep around the scarf.

Turn the scarf right side out, fold the cut edges in, and sew the bottom seams.

Wash and block the scarf (see page 28).

Fingerless Mittens

Knit a pair of coordinating fingerless mittens with leftover yarn from the *Geometric Dazzle Floppy Hat* and *Reversible Scarf*. Wear them alone or over store-bought black wool gloves. (Shown at right knit in Knit Picks Telemark yarn.)

Yarn Light Weight Yarn (CYCA 3), approx. 100 yd. each of Green, Rust, Gold, Gray, and Black or use leftover yarns from the **Geometric Dazzle Floppy Hat** or **Geometric Dazzle Reversible Scarf**.

Yarn Weight Sport, Light (CYCA 3)

Needles Size 5 (U.S.)/3.75 mm DPNs, or size needed to obtain gauge

Large-eye blunt needle

Stitch markers

2 safety pins

Pattern Sizes Child (Women's, Men's)

Measurements Width at Hand (not including thumb): 3⅛ in. (3¾ in., 4⅛ in.); Length: 6½ in. (7¾ in., 8¼ in.)

Pattern Difficulty Easy

Fair Isle Gauge 6.5 sts = 1 in., 8 rnds = 1 in. on size 5 needles

Note *See Taking the Fear Out of Fair Isle, page 23 for stranding instructions.*

Note *Choose any Fair Isle borders from the Geometric Dazzle Floppy Hat and Scarf Chart, in any order, for the Fingerless Mittens. If you are using leftover yarns, substitute ribbing colors as needed if you don't have enough of the suggested color.*

Knitting Instructions (make 2)

With Gold and size 5 DPNs, CO 40 (48, 56) sts. Without twisting the sts, join.

Cuff

Work 4 rnds each in K2, P2 ribbing in the following colors: Gold, Green, Rust, Gray, Black, or in the colors you desire.

PALM RND 1

K 1 rnd Black.

PALM RNDS 2-5

Select any border from the **Geometric Dazzle Floppy Hat and Reversible Scarf Chart**. Work the first 4 rnds of that chart.

THUMB GUSSET RND 1

With the background color, if it is a 2-color rnd, pick up and K 1 st, place marker, work rem of rnd according to the established border chart.

THUMB GUSSET RND 2

With the opposite color if it is a 2-color rnd, K 1, move marker, work rem of rnd according to the established border chart.

THUMB GUSSET RND 3

With the background color, if it is a 2-color rnd, pick up and K 1 st, work rem st in alternate color, pick up and K 1 st with background color, move marker, work rem of rnd according to the established border chart.

THUMB GUSSET RND 4

Work the sts before the marker in alternating colors if it is a 2-color rnd, move marker, work rem of rnd according to the established border chart.

Rep Thumb Gusset Rnds 3–4, alternating the st color of the gusset sts on 2-color rnds, until there are 13 (15, 17) sts before the marker.

Work 2 (4, 6) rnds even in the established border chart motif.

Hand

Place the 13 (15, 17) thumb sts divided on 2 safety pins, work rem of rnd according to the established border chart.

Work 2 (4, 6) rnds even in the established border chart motif.

Upper Ribbing

Work 4 rnds K2, P2 ribbing in Gold, or desired leftover yarn color. BO loosely.

Thumb

Place the 13 (15, 17) sts divided as evenly as possible on 3 DPNs.

THUMB RND 1

With Gold, or desired leftover yarn color, pick up and K 1, K rem of rnd. (14, 16, 18 sts)

THUMB RIBBING, CHILD'S AND MEN'S SIZES

Work 4 rnds K1, P1 ribbing. BO loosely.

THUMB RIBBING, WOMEN'S SIZE

Work 4 rnds K2, P2 ribbing. BO loosely.

Weave all ends in on the inside of the mittens. Wash and block mittens (see page 28).

Nordic Snowflake hat
and gloves, pattern on
pages 12 and 14.

Hat

This wonderful motif is an update of the classic snowflake pattern, traditionally used for pullovers. Soft, Alpaca fiber yarn would be ideal for this project. (Shown on page 11 knit in Decadent Fibers Marshmallow yarn.)

Yarn	Fine Weight Yarn (CYCA 2), approx. 100 yd. each of Natural, Light Gold, Dark Gold, Light Gray, Dark Gray
Yarn Weight	Sport Weight, Fine (CYCA 2)
Needles	Size 3 (U.S.)/3.25 mm 16-in. circular, size 3 (U.S.)/3.25 mm DPNs, or size needed to obtain gauge
	Large stitch markers
	Small stitch markers
	Large-eye blunt needle

Pattern Sizes	Child (Adult Small, Adult Large)
Note	*Adult Small and Adult Large are knit with the same number of stitches. The difference in sizes is in the length of the hat. Work both sizes as for Adult until noted in pattern.*
Measurements	Circumference: 15⅛ in. (19 in.); Length: 7¼ in. (8 in., 8¾ in.)
Pattern Difficulty	Easy
Fair Isle Gauge	7.5 sts = 1 in., 8 rnds = 1 in. on size 3 needles
Note	*For more about stranding, see Taking the Fear Out of Fair Isle, page 23.*

Nordic Snowflake Hat Chart 1

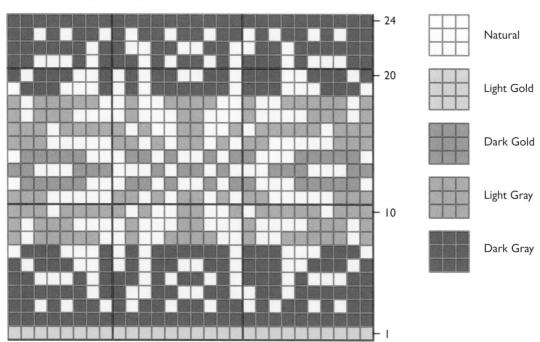

Natural

Light Gold

Dark Gold

Light Gray

Dark Gray

Knitting Instructions

With size 3 circular needle and Light Gray, CO 112 (140) sts. Without twisting sts, place marker, and join.

ALL SIZES
Work 8 rnds K1, P1 ribbing.

ALL SIZES
Work **Nordic Snowflake Hat Chart 1**, placing markers between reps if desired.

CHILD AND ADULT SMALL SIZE
Work Light Gray/Dark Gold border from **Nordic Snowflake Hat Chart 2**.

ADULT LARGE SIZE
Work Light Gray/Dark Gold border from **Nordic Snowflake Hat Chart 3**.

CHILD SIZE ONLY
With Light Gray, K next rnd, dec 2 sts evenly spaced in rnd. (110 sts rem)

CHILD DECREASE RND 1
K9, K2tog, rep around. (100 sts rem)

CHILD DECREASE RND 2, AND ALL EVEN RNDS
K.

CHILD DECREASE RND 3
K8, K2tog, rep around. (90 sts rem)

CHILD DECREASE RND 5
K7, K2tog, rep around. (80 sts rem)

CHILD DECREASE RND 7
K6, K2tog, rep around. (70 sts rem)

CHILD DECREASE RND 9
K5, K2tog, rep around. (60 sts rem)

CHILD DECREASE RND 11
K4, K2tog, rep around. (50 sts rem)

CHILD DECREASE RND 13
K3, K2tog, rep around. (40 sts rem)

CHILD DECREASE RND 15
K2, K2tog*, rep around. (30 sts rem)

CHILD DECREASE RND 17
K1, K2tog, rep around. (20 sts rem)

CHILD DECREASE RND 19
K2tog, rep around. (10 sts rem)

ADULT SMALL SIZE ONLY
With Light Gray, K 2 rnds even.

ADULT LARGE SIZE ONLY
With Light Gray, K 6 rnds even.

ADULT DECREASE RND 1
K12, K2tog, rep around. (130 sts rem)

ADULT DECREASE RND 2, AND ALL EVEN DECREASE RNDS
K.

ADULT DECREASE RND 3
K11, K2tog, rep around. (120 sts rem)

ADULT DECREASE RND 5
K10, K2tog, rep around. (110 sts rem)

Continue dec as for Child Size, beginning at Child Decrease Rnd 1.

Cut yarn, leaving a 10-in. tail. Thread the tail in a large-eye needle, and weave it through the remaining loops. Tighten and tie off. Weave all loose ends in on the inside of the hat. Wash and block hat.

Nordic Snowflake Hat Chart 2

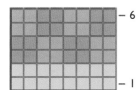

Nordic Snowflake Hat Chart 3

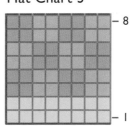

Gloves

This is a great pattern for new Fair Isle knitters—and it is also good for using up leftover yarn. Though designed for men, the smaller size should fit most women. (Shown at right knit in Decadent Fibers Marshmallow yarn.)

Yarn	Fine Weight Yarn (CYCA 2), approx. 100 yd. each of Natural, Light Gold, Dark Gold, Light Gray, Dark Gray
Yarn Weight	Sport Weight, Fine (CYCA 2)
Needles	Size 3 (U.S.)/3.25 mm and size 4 (U.S.)/3.5 mm DPNs, or size needed to obtain gauge
	Large stitch markers
	Small stitch markers
	8 safety pins
	Large-eye blunt needle
Pattern Sizes	Women's (Men's)
Measurements	All Sizes: Cuff: 3¾ in. long; Hand Width: 3⅜ in. (4 in.)

Pattern Difficulty	Intermediate
Fair Isle Gauge	7.5 sts = 1 in., 8 rnds = 1 in. on size 4 needles
Note	*For more about stranding, see Taking the Fear Out of Fair Isle, page 23.*

Knitting Instructions (make 2)

Note Regardless of size, when you complete the *Nordic Snowflake Hat & Glove Chart 1*, work 1 rnd of Light Gold, and then change to Dark Gold for the remainder of the glove.

With size 3 DPNs and Dark Gold, CO 50 (60) sts. Without twisting sts, join.

ALL SIZES

Work 30 rnds K1, P1 ribbing.

NEXT RND (ALL SIZES)

Change to size 4 DPNs, K around, placing a marker after st 25 (30).

WOMEN'S HAND RND 1

Beginning at square 3 of Rnd 1 of **Nordic Snowflake Hat & Glove Chart 1**, work chart to marker (3 squares will be left unworked), move marker, rep.

For rem of **Chart 1**, work as above, beginning each rnd of the chart at square 3, ending with 3 squares unworked (25-st rep), on both sides of the glove.

MEN'S HAND RND 1

K1 in the background color, work Rnd 1 of **Nordic Snowflake Hat & Glove Chart 1**, K1 in the background color, move marker, rep.

For rem of chart, work as above, beginning each rnd with a st in the background color, move marker, work each rnd of the chart, K1 in the background color, move marker, rep.

ALL SIZES

Work 3 more rnds even.

THUMB GUSSET RND 1 (ALL SIZES)

Pick up and K 1 in the background color, place marker, work rnd in established patt, following chart for your size.

THUMB GUSSET RND 2 (ALL SIZES)

Work st before marker in alternate color (if a 2-color rnd), move marker, work rnd in established patt, following chart for your size.

THUMB GUSSET RND 3 (ALL SIZES)

Pick up and K 1 st, K to marker, pick up and K 1 st, alternating colors on 2-color rnds, move marker, work rnd in established patt, following chart for your size.

THUMB GUSSET RND 4 (ALL SIZES)

Work sts before marker in alternate colors if a 2-color rnd, move marker, work rnd in established patt following chart for your size.

Rep Thumb Gusset Rnds 3–4 until there are 17 (21) sts before the marker in the thumb gusset.

ALL SIZES

Work 4 rnds even in established patt, following chart for your size.

HAND RND 1

Place the thumb gusset sts on 2 safety pins, and work the remainder of the rnd in the established patt (continuing with the chart if necessary, or with solid Dark Gold). (50, 60 sts)

Work 5 (7) more rnds even.

Note Work Fingers and Thumb with Dark Gold.

Divide for Fingers

K25 (30). Divide the sts on 2 needles. Beginning at the thumb side on the front needle, place the first 7 (8) sts on a safety pin for the front of the index finger. Place the next 6 (7) sts on a safety pin for the front of the middle finger. Place the next 6 (7) sts on a safety pin for the front of the ring finger. Rep with the sts on the back needle, beginning at the thumb side with the index finger.

Little Finger

Divide the rem 14 (16) sts on 3 needles. CO 2 sts in the gap between the front and the back. (16, 18 sts)

Work even until finger measures 1¾ in. (2¼ in.) long, or until the finger is ¼ in. shorter than desired length for each finger instruction.

LITTLE FINGER DECREASE RND

K2tog, rep around.

Cut yarn, leaving a 10-in. tail, and thread in a large-eye needle. Weave tail through remaining loops. Tighten and tie off on the inside of the glove.

Ring Finger

Place the 6 (7) front sts on a needle, place the 6 (7) back sts on a needle. Beginning at the little finger, pick up

2 sts along the edge of the little finger, K sts on needle, CO 2 sts in the gap. Redistribute sts on 3 needles. (16, 18 sts)

Work even until finger measures 2½ in. (3 in.) long. Dec and tie off as for Little Finger.

Middle Finger

Work as for Ring Finger until finger measures 3 in. (3½ in.) long. Dec and tie off as for Little Finger. (16, 18 sts)

Index Finger

Divide the sts on 3 needles. Beginning at the Middle Finger edge, pick up 2 sts along the edge. (14, 18 sts) Work as for Little Finger until finger measures 2¾ in. (3¼ in.) long. Dec and tie off as for Little Finger.

Thumb

Divide the 17 (21) sts on 3 needles. Pick up and K 1 st in the gap between the thumb and the hand. (18, 22 sts) Work even until Thumb measures 1½ in. (2⅛ in.) long.

THUMB DECREASE RND 1
K2tog, rep around. (9, 11 sts)

THUMB DECREASE RND 2
K.

THUMB DECREASE RND 3
K2tog, rep around, end with K1.
Tighten and tie off as for Little Finger.
Weave all ends in on the inside of the gloves. Use the tails to close any gaps between the fingers. Wash and block gloves.

Nordic Snowflake Hat & Glove Chart

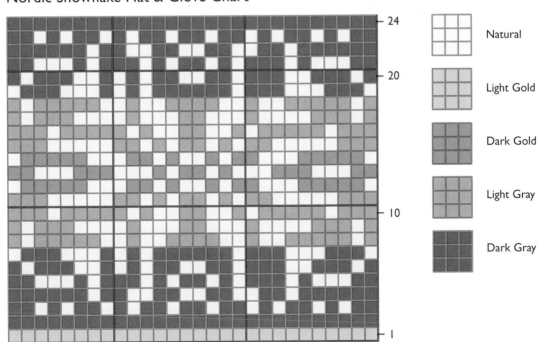

Natural	
Light Gold	
Dark Gold	
Light Gray	
Dark Gray	

Women's Mittens

These wonderful matching mittens have motifs that represent life on the prairie: wheat fields, pheasants (the ring-necked pheasant is South Dakota's state bird), and the ever-present thistles. (Shown at right knit in Knit Picks Palette™ yarn.)

Yarn Superfine Weight Yarn (CYCA 1), approx. 100 yd. each of Ivory, Brown, Tan, Green, Red, Blue, and Dark Gray

Yarn Weight Fingering, Superfine (CYCA 1)

Needles Size 2 (U.S.)/3 mm DPNs or 1 or 2 long circulars, as desired

Large-eye blunt needle

Stitch markers

2 safety pins

Pattern Sizes Women's Average (Women's Large)

Note *Women's Average will fit most youth sizes. Shorten cuff and hand as needed for proper fit.*

Measurements Width: 3½ in. (4 in.); Length: 11 in. (11½ in.)

Pattern Difficulty Intermediate

Fair Isle Gauge 9 sts = 1 in., 10 rnds = 1 in.

Note *For more about stranding, see Taking the Fear Out of Fair Isle, page 23.*

Knitting Instructions (make 2)

With size 2 DPNs and Green, CO 64 (72 sts). Divide sts on 3 or 4 DPNs or 1 or 2 circular needles as desired. Without twisting sts, place marker, and join.

RIBBING

Work 6 rnds K2, P2 ribbing.

NEXT RND

K32 (36), place marker, K to end of rnd.

Note

For Women's Average, work **Dakota Dreams Mittens Charts** as shown for each rep throughout (32 sts). For Women's Large, work 2 sts in background color (on 2-color rnds), work **Dakota Dreams Mittens Charts** as shown, work 2 sts in background color (on 2-color rnds), for each rep throughout (36 sts). For both sizes, work **Dakota Dreams Mittens Chart 1**, followed by **Dakota Dreams Mittens Chart 2**, then work **Chart 1** again.

Following charts in the order instructed above, work until cuff measures 4½ in. for all sizes.

THUMB GUSSET RND 1

Following chart as instructed, pick up and K 1 st in the background color (if a 2-color rnd), place marker, finish rnd in established manner following chart.

THUMB GUSSET RND 2

Following chart as instructed, K1 in the alternate color (if a 2-color rnd), move marker, finish rnd in established manner following chart.

THUMB GUSSET RND 3

Alternating colors throughout the gusset on 2-color rnds (until you get to the border above the Pheasant Border on **Chart 3**, which is worked as shown on the chart), pick up and K 1 st, work thumb gusset to marker, pick up and K 1 st, move marker, finish rnd in established manner following chart.

THUMB GUSSET RND 4

Alternating colors throughout the gusset on 2-color rnds (except as noted), work sts to marker, move marker, finish rnd in established manner, following chart. Rep Thumb Gusset Rnds 3–4 until there are 19 (21) sts before the marker.

Work 5 (7) rnds even in the established manner, following chart.

HAND RND 1

Place the thumb gusset sts on 2 safety pins, work rnd in established manner, following chart. (64, 72 sts)
Work hand in established manner, following chart until hand measures 3¼ in. (3½ in.) or to the end of the little finger.

Note Work all decs in background color on 2-color rnds.

DECREASE RND

K2tog TBL, work in established manner until there are 2 sts before the marker, K2tog, move marker, rep around.
Rep Decrease Rnd until there are 24 (28) sts left, working last 4 rnds in a solid color.
Divide sts evenly on 2 needles, front and back, and turn mitten inside out. Work a three-needle bind-off to close the end of the mitten.
Cut yarn, and tie off. Turn mitten right side out.

Thumb

Divide the 19 (21) sts evenly on DPNs or circular needles as desired. Following established chart, pick up and K 1 st in the gap with the background color on a 2-color rnd. (20, 22 sts)
Continue working **Chart 1** in established manner, and then alternate Green and Tan sts, until thumb measures 2 in. (2¼ in.).

THUMB DECREASE RND 1

With Tan, *K2tog*, rep around. (10, 11 sts rem).

THUMB DECREASE RND 2

K2tog, rep around, ending with K1 for Women's Large.
Cut yarn, leaving a 10-in. tail. Thread tail in a large-eye blunt needle, and weave through remaining sts. Tighten and tie off on the inside of the mitten. Weave all loose ends in on the inside of the mitten. Wash and block mitten.

Dakota Dreams Mittens Chart 1

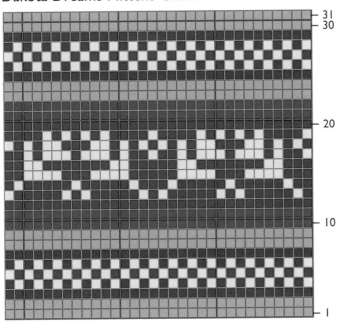

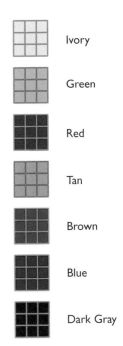

Ivory

Green

Red

Tan

Brown

Blue

Dark Gray

Dakota Dreams Mittens Chart 2

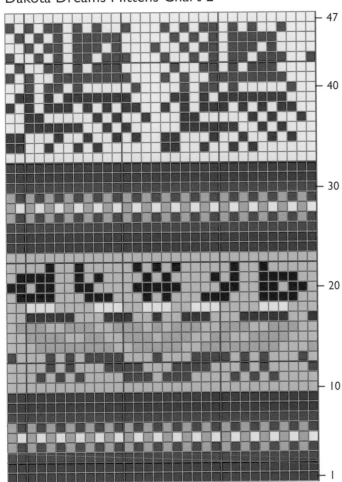

Men's Hat

The *Dakota Dreams* hat pattern is worked in golds, browns, and rusts: the colors beautifully represent South Dakota at harvest with fall on the way and winter following close behind. (Pictured below knit in Knit Picks Palette yarn.)

Yarn	Superfine Weight Yarn (CYCA 1), approx. 100 yd. each of Black, Brown, Tan, Rust, Gold, Ivory, and Gray	**Pattern Size**	One size fits all
Yarn Weight	Fingering, Superfine (CYCA 1)	**Measurements**	Hat Circumference: 20 in.; Hat Length: 8 in.
Needles	Size 2 (U.S.)/3 mm 16-in. circulars; size 3 (U.S.)/3.25 mm DPNs, 16-in. circulars	**Pattern Difficulty**	Easy
	Large-eye blunt needle	**Fair Isle Gauge**	8 sts = 1 in., 10 rnds = 1 in. on size 3 needles
	Assorted stitch markers	**Note**	*For more about stranding, see Taking the Fear Out of Fair Isle, page 23.*

Knitting Instructions

With 16-in. size 2 circular needle and Black, CO 160 sts. Place a marker and without twisting the sts, join.

RNDS 1–2

Work K2, P2 ribbing.

Corrugated Ribbing Rnds 3–12

Work all K2 sts with black, alternating colors for the P2 sts in this order, 2 rnds each: Brindle Heather, Camel Heather, Masala, Turmeric, Oyster Heather.

NEXT RND

Change to size 3 circular needle, K with Black.

Work **Dakota Dreams Hat Chart 2**, followed by **Chart 1**, placing a marker between each rep.

When hat measures 6½ in., begin decs.

DECREASE RND

Continuing in charted patt, *K2tog, work to within 2 sts of marker, K2tog TBL, move marker*, rep around. On 2-color rnds, work the decs in the background color regardless of which color is indicated on the chart for that st. Change to DPNs as desired.

Work the decs every rnd until 10 sts rem. Cut yarn, leaving a 10-in. tail. Thread the tail in a large-eye needle, and pull through the remaining loops. Tighten and tie off on the inside of the hat. Weave all loose ends in. Wash and block hat (see page 28).

Dakota Dreams Hat Chart 1

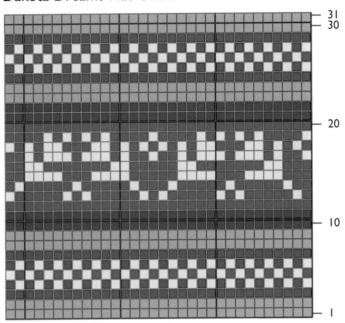

31
30

20

10

1

Ivory

Gold

Rust

Tan

Brown

Gray

Black

Dakota Dreams Hat Chart 2

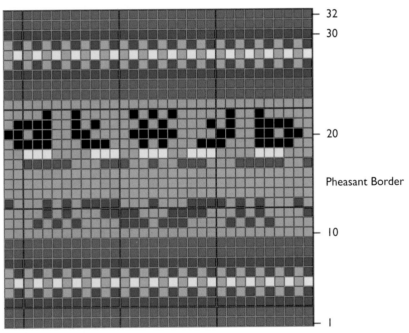

32
30

20

Pheasant Border

10

1

Taking the Fear Out of Fair Isle

Take a deep breath and repeat after me:

"Fair Isle is fabulous. Fair Isle is fun. Fair Isle is easy. I am not afraid."

Yeah, you heard me: Knitting Fair Isle is easy. It's fun. And it can be fearless, whether you're using just two yarns or going wild with forty.

If you're new to stranded knitting, we'll walk you through the basics: yarn selection, swatching, tension, and the bugaboo of all beginning Fair Islers steeking. You'll learn traditional methods for knitting Fair Isle designs, and you'll learn some not-so-traditional techniques, which will take the mystery, and the fear, out of colorwork.

Newbies can get their Fair Isle feet wet with easy patterns that need no steeking, like mittens and hats. Advanced stranded knitters will love our beautiful patterns and charts. And adventurous knitters will find ways to simplify their Fair Isle knitting even more.

I promise, you will learn to cut your knitting fearlessly.

What Is Fair Isle, Anyway?

Technically, Fair Isle knitting is multicolored stranded work, done in traditional patterns that originated in the Fair Isle, near the Orkneys and Shetland Islands. Most knitters use the term "Fair Isle" to describe any stranded, multicolor knitting.

Whatever you call it, Fair Isle knitting is not as complex as it looks. In any given row or round, you are only working with two colors, and you are only actually knitting with one color at a time, switching colors on individual stitches according to a predetermined pattern, which is usually drawn on a grid or chart.

Choose your yarns carefully. In any Fair Isle or stranded project, it is very important for the two yarn colors that you are using (in any given row) to have a high contrast. If you can't easily see the difference between the colors before you knit them, you won't see the difference afterward.

Of course, the recommended yarns will work just fine for the designs in this book. But if you plan to substitute yarns, a good way to know if your yarns have enough contrast for stranding is to photograph or scan your yarns together, and then turn the picture into a black-and-white image (see the bottom photo on the facing page). If you can still tell which yarn is which, then your color contrast is sufficient.

Choose firm, evenly spun and/or plied yarns, with little or no halo or fuzziness or bumps, so that the pattern in your finished fabric will be crisp and visible. Some tweediness is okay for stranding. If you select self-striping or variegated yarns (either paired together, or with a solid-color yarn) make sure that *all* of the colors in your striping or variegated yarn contrast highly with the color(s) of the other yarn.

If you are substituting yarns for a pattern that uses steeks, or cutting, select yarns with some *grab:* wool or wool blends. Those yarns, even the superwash versions, will hold on to each other and help prevent raveling when the steeks are cut. Some all-wool yarns, such as the Shetland varieties, are known for adhering so well that traditionalists do not reinforce the cut edges at all.

Yarns that are very slippery (such as pure cotton, pure silk, and many man-made fibers) can be used for steeked projects, but the chance of raveling after cutting is much higher. I do not ever recommend cutting slippery yarns without reinforcing the steek edge first.

Swatches? Really?

Okay, there's fearless. And then there's foolish.

It is totally foolish to knit a large Fair Isle project without first knitting a swatch, not only to test your gauge against the listed pattern gauge (recommended needle sizes are just that—recommendations—and you may need to go up or down one or more needle sizes to get the same gauge in your knitting), but also to make sure that the colors look good together and that they have enough contrast to make stranding worth the effort.

And even more important, you want to be absolutely certain that your yarn colors won't bleed. Trust me, you do not want to spend months knitting a red and white Fair Isle sweater only to have it become pink and pinker after washing.

In addition, the gauges listed in this book are measured and calculated *after* the fabric has been wet-blocked. Washing and blocking changes not only the look and texture of the yarn, but it can also change the final gauge and measurements.

Knit a swatch. Wash it. Block it. And dry it. You'll be glad you did.

In the pages that follow, I'll show you the essentials of knitting Fair Isle patterns. You'll read all about changing yarn colors, knitting from a chart, holding the yarn strands for the floats, wet blocking, laundering, steeking, and shaping. It sounds like a lot, but it's simpler than you can imagine.

Happy knitting,
KATHLEEN TAYLOR

Increases and Decreases

Let's start with knitting increases and decreases, which is something that tends to bedevil beginners. The experienced among you may have your own approach, so do what you know to work best.

Increases

I like to increase stitches by picking up and knitting the side loop from the stitch in the row directly below the row I am working on. This increase does not leave a hole in my knitting. There are other types of increases. Use the one that you prefer, but be consistent. Use the same increase throughout.

Left-Slanting Decreases

Unless otherwise noted, any decrease indicated on the right side of a chart will be a left-slanting decrease. In other words, it's a decrease where the combined stitches lean toward the left.

The slip, slip, knit (SSK), in which you slip the first stitch as if to knit, slip the second stitch as if to knit, then slide the left-hand needle into the front part of both stitches and knit them together, makes a nice left-slanting decrease.

You may use an SSK for any left-slanting decrease in this book. However, I prefer to knit two together through the back loop (K2tog TBL), which produces the same effect with less effort. Simply slip your right needle into the back side of the two stitches, and knit them together. Whether you use an SSK or a K2tog TBL, be consistent. Use the same left-slanting decrease throughout any given project.

Right-Slanting Decreases

Unless otherwise noted, any decrease indicated on the left side of a chart will be a right-slanting decrease. In other words, it's a decrease where the combined stitches lean toward the right. Work all right-slanting decreases by knitting two stitches together in the usual way (K2tog).

Changing Yarn Colors the Fearless Way

There are many "official" ways to change yarn colors at the beginning of a round, which is where you switch colors on most Fair Isle projects. The fearless way is just to cut the former color, leaving at least a 3-in. tail. Then tie the new color to the old color with a plain old square knot, leaving at least a 3-in. tail on the new yarn color, and continue knitting.

That square knot will loosen a bit as your knitting progresses, and sometimes the first and last stitches of those rounds will look a little loose as well. Don't worry about them.

After you finish your project, when it comes time to weave your loose ends in (the ends that aren't trimmed off when the steek is cut open, that is), use a needle to further loosen and untie the knot, pull on the ends a bit to tighten the adjacent stitches, and retie the square knot firmly. Then weave the ends in along the wrong side of the knitted row for an inch or so, and trim the excess tail.

I have never had a knot tied in this manner come undone in wearing or washing. The small knots don't show from the front of the fabric, nor do they make lumps on the wrong side (in socks, for instance).

An added bonus is that tightening the yarn ends often makes that "jog" that happens at the beginning of color-change rounds disappear entirely.

Speaking of that Jog

There are ways to eliminate the jogs that occur at the beginning of a round of striped or Fair Isle knitting. I don't worry about them—I consider them the nature of the beast.

Joining Same-Color Yarns the Fearless Way

If you need to join more yarn to a same-color round (for example, if you're working on a project with large areas of single color), you can tie the yarn ends together, as listed above.

But even more fearlessly, if you are using a yarn that can be felted (wool or wool blends that are not superwash), you can *spit-join* your yarn ends together.

I know this sounds a bit ooky, but it works: Put the end of the old yarn and the end of the new yarn in your mouth (just go with me here), and roll them around for a moment or two. Get them good and wet. Take the yarns out of your mouth, overlap the ends a couple of inches lengthwise, and squeeze them together to form a single strand. Place the strand with the wet portion on one palm. Place the other palm on top and rub your hands together vigorously until the yarn strands felt together (you can feel when that happens).

Then just knit. The join will hold. I promise. In addition, felting reduces the bulk of that short area of double stranding. It won't show from the front (or back) of your work. And once the yarn dries, you'll never be able to find the join again.

If you're really squeamish, you can wet the yarn ends with tap water, but that means getting up and going to the sink. It's easier to do it the totally fearless way.

Yarn Dominance and Ball Placement

It is important in Fair Isle knitting to pick up your strands in the same order throughout your project. I place my main or background color (MC) on the right arm of my chair or beside me, and the contrast color (CC) on the floor or in my lap in front of me, and keep that placement throughout. I am a "thrower." I have learned that some "pickers" prefer to place the CC on the arm of their chair, and the MC in front. Do whatever works for you, but be consistent. Don't change the placement of the balls in the middle of the project.

There are some Fair Isle knitters who twist the yarns around each other on every stitch. I don't recommend that—it not only takes time and uses up a lot more yarn, but the resulting fabric is stiff.

Do not twist the strands around each other unless you are knitting more than five to seven stitches of the same color in a row on the chart, depending on the yarn weight. You can go up to seven stitches with fingering weight yarn without twisting the strands. If you do have to twist the yarns in the middle of long stretches of the same color, untwist them on the next stitch, so that the original ball placement/strand orientation returns. Your finished piece will have uniform stitching and color "dominance" if you maintain the same strand order throughout.

Knitting from a Chart

Each square on a Fair Isle chart represents one stitch. The color of the square represents the color yarn you are supposed to use for that stitch.

Each pattern will specify where to begin on the chart. Some projects begin at the top row, right-hand square of the chart. Others begin at the bottom row, right-hand square of the chart.

Some sizes of some patterns will indicate a different place to begin your first pattern repeat. Individual instructions will specify where to begin working those charts.

One row of squares on the chart equals one repeat of the motif. Each time you finish a repeat of your pattern round, go back to the first stitch and start over for the next pattern repeat on your round.

I find it extremely helpful to place markers between each repeat. That way, if I make a mistake, I only have to go back to the beginning of the repeat to find the error.

Each row of squares on the chart represents one round of knitting. When you finish one complete round of repeats, begin the next round on the far right square in the row up (or down, depending on where you started working) from the one you just completed.

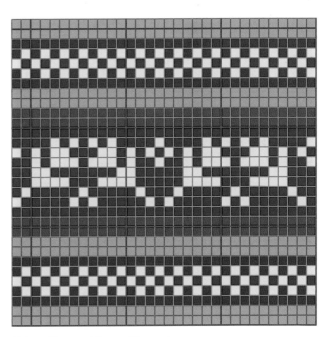

Dakota Dreams Mittens Chart

I don't just find it helpful to mark which round I am knitting on a chart, I find it absolutely essential to do so. There is no chart so simple that I cannot lose my place in it, thereby causing angst and anguish, wasted work, and many bad words. I eliminate that possibility by using a metal sheet and strip magnets to highlight the chart row I am working on, with the magnetic strip placed just above my current row. If you don't have a metal sheet and strip magnets, you may use sticky notes in the same way. You can also photocopy the chart and use a highlighter to draw through each completed row.

Charted Decreases

Some project charts have decreases built right into them. Those charts look something like a pyramid, with the numbers of squares (and stitches) in a repeat gradually diminishing. The charts will have clearly visible jogs on decrease rounds. Each decrease is represented by a clearly delineated jog in the chart. When you come to a jog, you simply decrease one stitch (with either a K2tog TBL or a K2tog, depending on the side of the chart where the decrease falls), using the yarn color shown in the square.

Each decrease reduces the number of stitches in the repeat (and therefore in the entire project).

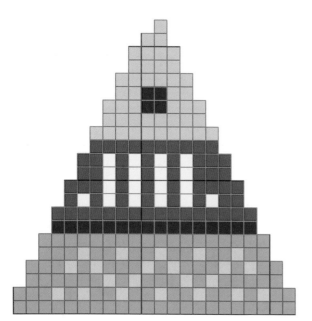

The decreases are built right into the charts for some Fair Isle patterns.

Changing to Double-Pointed Needles

Unless you are using the Magic Loop method, or are knitting with two long circular needles, as you work on any pattern with decreases, you will have to switch from longer circular needles to shorter ones, and from circular needles to double-pointed needles (DPNs). Or, conversely, if you are working from the cuff up, on sleeves, for example, you'll start with DPNs and then switch to circulars as the stitch count increases. Use whatever circular length feels comfortable to you (changing them as necessary), and switch over to DPNs as needed.

If at all possible, place an entire pattern repeat (or multiple repeats) on separate DPNs. Be aware that your tension and gauge may change a bit in the switch to DPNs. If you find yourself knitting tighter on DPNs, move up a needle size.

Holding the Yarn Strands for the Floats

There are many ways to hold the yarn strands in Fair Isle knitting. The one that is correct is the one that works best for you. I hold both strands of yarn in my right hand. Other knitters hold one strand in their left hand and one in their right. However you hold your yarn, arrange the yarn balls as instructed earlier.

For beginners, I recommend holding only the strand that you are knitting with. When you finish the stitches for that color, drop that strand and pick up the other and knit those stitches without twisting the yarns around each other. After you feel comfortable switching colors, try holding both of the strands in one hand, or one strand in each hand. Experiment until you find the method that feels the most comfortable to you.

Float Tension

It takes practice to achieve even float tension when Fair Isle knitting. As mentioned above, I find it easiest for beginners to hold only the strand they're actually knitting with, then drop that strand and pick up the next color (as indicated on the chart), and loosely pull it up to the needle and continue knitting.

Even the best Fair Isle knitters get some puckering—don't worry if you see some in your work. As long as your knitting will stretch (test the elasticity occasionally), you should be able to block the puckers out. As you knit and get used to the process, you will find that your float tension relaxes on its own.

Twisting the Yarn Strands in the Float

Unless you are knitting a stretch of more than five to seven stitches of the same color in a motif, it is not necessary to twist the yarn strands around each other as you knit. If you do knit more than five to seven stitches in the same color on a row, at about the middle of that section of stitches, twist the "live" yarn around the "other" strand once and knit a stitch. Then untwist the yarn and continue on. This method produces a nicely elastic fabric, with a good drape.

It is common for a hint of the twisted stitch to show from the front of the fabric. If the chart has large areas of single-color stretches that extend over several rows of squares, stagger your twisted stitches so that they're not directly above or below each other to lessen their visibility on the right side of the work.

Weaving In the Ends

If your project involves steeking, many of your yarn ends will be cut away and discarded when the steek is cut open. (Yay!)

But for sleeves knit one at a time, and for pullover sweaters and vests, as well as hats, mittens, and socks—that is, for any tube that is not cut open—every color change involves yarn ends that will have to be woven in. It's boring, but it has to be done.

After retying the knots, thread one yarn end in a large-eye blunt needle (choose a needle that is only as big as it needs to be to fit the yarn through the eye). Working horizontally along a nearby row of stitches, on the wrong side of the fabric, weave the yarn end over and under several of the purl bumps (or over and under adjacent floats). Do this for about an inch. Trim the yarn end.

Repeat until you are finished with all of the yarn ends, or until you run screaming into the night, whichever happens first.

Weaving in ends

Wet Blocking

Wet blocking allows your yarns to bloom, stretch, and even out for a beautiful finished project. There are many products specifically produced for blocking and washing hand knits, but I use dish soap.

To wet-block small items, run a sink full of hot water. Add a small amount of dish soap and stir it around until the water is mildly sudsy. Submerge your item in the hot, soapy water, and allow it to soak for at least a half hour. Do not agitate the item, unless you want it to felt. Drain the water, and rinse in clear water no cooler than the soaking water. Gently squeeze the excess moisture from the item (rolled up in a towel), or put it in the spin cycle of your washing machine (do not agitate). After the excess moisture has been removed, smooth your item out. You may be able to just smooth it to the proper dimensions given in the pattern. Smooth the fabric, tug at any puckers, pull edges and sides even. Be sure to check the front, back, top, and bottom of the item, and smooth and tug as needed.

When it meets your approval, simply lay it flat somewhere and allow it to air-dry (I usually leave everything, from socks to sweaters, on top of my dryer overnight).

If the item will not smooth or unpucker properly, you may stretch the fabric, and then use nonrusting pins. When I pin-block an item, I usually just pin it to my living-room rug (as long as I know that the yarn that will not bleed or run). You may want to invest in a blocking board.

Be careful when pinning your item—any portions pulled out of shape will remain that way after the pins are removed. Allow the item to dry and remove the pins.

To wet-block large items, repeat the above steps, soaking the item in the washing machine or a large bucket or basin, or even in the bathtub. Be very careful not to let the washer go into agitation.

It is possible to add about 10 percent to the height and width of a knitted item by careful blocking, so if your piece is too small, you can widen and lengthen it at this stage.

Blocking only lasts as long as the item remains dry. You will have to reblock your item every time it is washed or gets wet in any way.

Laundering

Even if your item has been knit with superwash wool that is absolutely machine washable and dryable, you'll want to launder it exactly as for the blocking process. Machine washing superwash Fair Isle items leaves them shapeless and lumpy.

Steeks

For knitting purposes, a steek is a built-in seam allowance, which allows knitters to make Fair Isle projects entirely in the round, without having to work back and forth or purl stranded designs. The steek is cut open after the knitting is finished and additional shaping is done (such as curved necklines) or pieces (like sleeves) are added.

The biggest fear a knitter has, when cutting that first steek, is that the fabric will unravel. I won't pretend that can't happen, but as long as you use the right kind of yarn (with some grab) and don't play tug-of-war with your freshly cut knitting, those steek stitches won't go anywhere you don't want them to go.

Yes, it's scary the first time you take scissors to your knitting. I will admit to drinking a glass of wine before I cut my first steek. These days, I don't even think about it (outside of measuring many times before cutting). The ease of working a sweater tube in the round far outweighs any fear of cutting into the knitting, which is a fabric, just like any other.

Steek Construction

Some knitters like to use an uneven number of stitches in their steeks, and then cut down the middle of the center stitch when they open the steek. I prefer to use an even number of stitches and cut between the center two stitches.

Center-front steeks, for cardigans, are built into the original number of cast-on stitches (the first and last five stitches of the round composing the steek). Regardless of any stitch patterning on the body of the sweater, including textured stitches, ribbing, or cables, the steek stitches are always plain knit stitches.

Armhole and V-neck steeks are added to the construction at the right spot in the knitting by casting on a set number of stitches. Those stitches then become the steek, and they are worked the same way a center-front steek is worked.

In all cases, work your steek stitches in alternate colors on two-color rounds, except for the center two stitches, which are worked in the same color to make them easier to identify when it comes time to reinforce the steeks for cutting.

Steek Reinforcement

CROCHETED STEEKS The advantage of a crocheted steek is that you don't need any complicated machinery to do the work for you. You can crochet a steek on the bus or while standing in line at the post office. The disadvantage of a crocheted steek is that the crocheted edge adds bulk to the steek.

To make a crocheted steek, find and mark the center row of stitches along the length of your steek (easy to discover if you have worked those center stitches in the same color, as recommended above). Using a contrasting fine yarn (smaller than the yarn used to knit the project) and a properly sized crochet hook, begin at the top, working a single crochet through the center of the middle stitch. Then work a single crochet from the center stitch, and one through the stitch directly beside it on the steek row. Continue making single crochets down the entire steek side. Cut and tie off the yarn, and repeat on the other side.

Picking Up Stitches

Many Fair Isle patterns have front and neck bands that are picked up and knit along folded steek edges. When you pick up a stitch, insert the left needle through both loops of the base stitch, and knit those loops with the right needle. The new stitch goes on the right needle, and is now live.

Pick up and knit the number of stitches instructed in each pattern.

Picking Up Stitches the Fearless Way

Except in a very few cases (buttonhole bands, for example, or bands that have Fair Isle patterning, or need multiples of four stitches for ribbing), it really doesn't matter if you pick up the exact number of stitches listed in the pattern for neck bands, armhole openings, or front bands. A few more or less won't make a difference.

While you can pick up one stitch for each horizontal stitch or vertical row in a piece of knitting, you can often get by with fewer stitches. A rule of thumb if you're not counting the picked-up stitches, is to pick up four stitches for each five rows of vertical knitting. Along horizontal stretches, four stitches for each five stitches works as well. It's a matter of guessing and judging when you pick up stitches along a curved neckline.

Do keep track of how many stitches you pick up on armholes and front bands, so that you pick up the same number on the other opening.

Picking up stitches for the shaped neckline along the basted line

Look for these other THREADS Selects booklets at www.taunton.com and wherever crafts are sold.

Baby Beanies
Debby Ware
EAN: 9781621137634
8 ½ x 10 ⅞, 32 pages
Product# 078001
$9.95 U.S., $11.95 Can.

Fair Isle Flower Garden
Kathleen Taylor
EAN: 9781621137702
8 ½ x 10 ⅞, 32 pages
Product# 078008
$9.95 U.S., $11.95 Can.

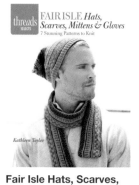

Fair Isle Hats, Scarves, Mittens & Gloves
Kathleen Taylor
EAN: 9781621137719
8 ½ x 10 ⅞, 32 pages
Product# 078009
$9.95 U.S., $11.95 Can.

Lace Socks
Kathleen Taylor
EAN: 9781621137894
8 ½ x 10 ⅞, 32 pages
Product# 078012
$9.95 U.S., $11.95 Can.

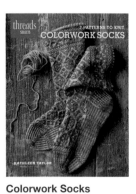

Colorwork Socks
Kathleen Taylor
EAN: 9781621137740
8 ½ x 10 ⅞, 32 pages
Product# 078011
$9.95 U.S., $11.95 Can.

DIY Bride Cakes & Sweets
Khris Cochran
EAN: 9781621137665
8 ½ x 10 ⅞, 32 pages
Product# 078004
$9.95 U.S., $11.95 Can.

DIY Bride Beautiful Bouquets
Khris Cochran
EAN: 9781621137672
8 ½ x 10 ⅞, 32 pages
Product# 078005
$9.95 U.S., $11.95 Can.

Bead Necklaces
Susan Beal
EAN: 9781621137641
8 ½ x 10 ⅞, 32 pages
Product# 078002
$9.95 U.S., $11.95 Can.

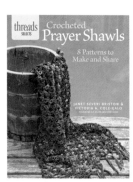

Drop Earrings
Susan Beal
EAN: 9781621137658
8 ½ x 10 ⅞, 32 pages
Product# 078003
$9.95 U.S., $11.95 Can.

Crochet Prayer Shawls
Janet Severi Bristow & Victoria A. Cole-Galo
EAN: 9781621137689
8 ½ x 10 ⅞, 32 pages
Product# 078006
$9.95 U.S., $11.95 Can.

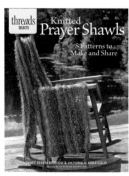

Knitted Prayer Shawls
Janet Severi Bristow & Victoria A. Cole-Galo
EAN: 9781621137696
8 ½ x 10 ⅞, 32 pages
Product# 078007
$9.95 U.S., $11.95 Can.

Shawlettes
Jean Moss
EAN: 9781621137726
8 ½ x 10 ⅞, 32 pages
Product# 078010
$9.95 U.S., $11.95 Can.